"Rhodes has cr
Manning's origin
response. There's
luminosity, too. V
voice is remarkably intimate as it addresses the source of
life—adversary, beloved, and mystery always. Gorgeous."

—C. E. MORGAN
Author of *The Sport of Kings*

"J. Stephen Rhodes is a fearless poet who dares to write with irony, humor, and humility about the wild, inscrutable God who is Boss. Reading him, one catches glimpses of an actual unposed devout life wrestling with the One who delights in our wrestling. His images are often wry, ironic displays of human spirit that is thoroughly enfleshed."

—ROY HOWARD
Presbyterian minister and
book editor at the *Presbyterian Outlook*

"Steve Rhodes's poetic sequence *Boss* begins, 'I went walking in the marsh / Boss the one with live oaks / dead pines cypress knees,' sweeping us into a spiritual journey that is field guide, psalter, cry, and song. This opening poem wonders 'was that you Boss / beneath cypress and tupelo.' In compact lines stripped to the essential, this human voice bluntly addresses a God who is elusive, mysterious, even bewildering, a trickster God whom the speaker knows to be the steadiest of companions."

—SUZANNE CLEARY
Author of *Crude Angel*

"The two best words to describe Steve Rhodes's poetry are *fresh* and *classic*. His ideas are rooted in sacred tradition yet painted with fresh insights for today's world of belief with its many challenges. Reading him is like returning to another time and place and then discovering you're living in the midst of today's realities."

—J. MICHAEL A. WRIGHT
Dean, Grace Church Cathedral,
Charleston, South Carolina

"Before I knew the poetry of J. Stephen Rhodes, I knew him as a theologian, educator, and an accidental farmer. I know the tract of land he owned in Kentucky. I even bush-hogged it a few times. But even if I had not already seen it, Rhodes's poems allow me to 'see' that landscape and others where he keeps up a running, honest, poignant, funny, and demanding conversation with Boss. I once read where Rowan Williams said every theologian is beginning in the middle of things. Rhodes's Boss poems are situated in the Middle, where an imperfect person attempts to have honest conversations with Boss. Rhodes unveils for his readers a landscape we can all see in order to show us the Boss who remains, as always, veiled, while also known."

—BRIAN COLE
Bishop, Episcopal Diocese of East Tennessee

Was That You Boss

Was That You Boss

J. STEPHEN RHODES

Foreword by J. Michael A. Wright

RESOURCE *Publications* · Eugene, Oregon

WAS THAT YOU BOSS

Copyright © 2021 J. Stephen Rhodes. All rights reserved. Except for brief quotations in critical publications or reviews, no part of this book may be reproduced in any manner without prior written permission from the publisher. Write: Permissions, Wipf and Stock Publishers, 199 W. 8th Ave., Suite 3, Eugene, OR 97401.

Resource Publications
An Imprint of Wipf and Stock Publishers
199 W. 8th Ave., Suite 3
Eugene, OR 97401

www.wipfandstock.com

PAPERBACK ISBN: 978-1-6667-0195-1
HARDCOVER ISBN: 978-1-6667-0196-8
EBOOK ISBN: 978-1-6667-0197-5

05/26/21

*For Maurice Manning
and Sally Rhoads*

*Am I not the whole? Am I not all things
when I weep, and you the single one
who hears it?*

—Rilke

FOREWORD

In the rustling grass I hear him pass,
He speaks to me everywhere.

These words from Maltbie D. Babcock's hymn, "This is my Father's World," began to sing out to me as I read Steve Rhodes' most recent collection of poems. One is not surprised to discover that Babcock's words were, in time, happily married to a tune named 'Terra Beata' (Blessed Earth). For Steve Rhodes, God's creation is just that, forever blessed and anointed as good and gift. Creation sings and signs in so many ways in this modern psalter. Steve captures the mood and carries on where those temple songs began many centuries ago. Before we know it, we are invited into the song as we encounter that same creation now more fully alive and ever ready to nurture us.

I'm not sure when pilgrims began to turn off the creation tap while in search of the Other, but thanks be to Boss, the spigot has opened and such fun and faith are now released for all to enjoy. I celebrate this creative enterprise as it reminds us all that landscape is Godscape, a place to be still and know what the psalmist taught us so very long ago.

As you read (pray) these words uttered from the mouth of my poet, pastor, teacher and friend, don't be surprised to find your own insights bubbling up from the creation that echoes constantly for all who would dare to listen.

The Very Reverend J. Michael A. Wright
Dean of Grace Church Cathedral, Charleston, S.C.

PREFACE

MY INITIAL IDEA TO address poems in the manner of this collection was triggered by Maurice Manning's remarkable poetry collection, *Bucolics*. In that collection Manning carries on an extended conversation with a being he calls "Boss"—a conversation that is at once playful and probing, yet somehow reverent. While the poems in my collection are also addressed to a being named "Boss," any similarities or differences in our conceptions of such a being are mostly functions of our individual personalities and viewpoints. I have not set out to write an extension or refutation of Manning's conception of his "Boss," but as best as I am able, simply to explore my own.

Like Manning, I had the great privilege of living on a Kentucky farm for a number of years, so the language of nature and agriculture that figures prominently in his poems also does so in my own. I cannot overstate how profoundly moved I was when I first discovered *Bucolics* a decade ago and how Manning's poems move me still, nor can I exaggerate how grateful I am to him for having opened an important door for me in the way I understand my own "Boss."

J. S. R.

1

I went walking in the marsh
Boss the one with live oaks
dead pines cypress knees
I went walking and heard
a song I couldn't name
not a chirp more a groan
was that you Boss
beneath cypress and tupelo
deep under duckweed
covering lagoons
was that you waking up
or an alligator in heat
you giving birth
to the new day
or a barred owl
in a hollow tree
maybe Boss maybe
you were just saying hello

2

Boss is that you
do you bend saplings
toss giant oaks
like birds that flee
then do you stop
like a cat who's decided
to lick herself clean
not making a leaf stir
do you let the dirt dry hard
then wash it all away
are you moody Boss
as I am when my ax head
breaks off or I trip
over a root
are you wild Boss
the way the earth is wild
oceans flat like a dinner plate
then whole villages drown
are you watching it all Boss
like me sitting on a stump
did you set free
wind water fire earth
like jaybirds off a tree
the way you did with me

3

are you against me Boss
the way the wind won't let me
open the front door
the way the ice locks
my eyelids shut
makes all the oaks groan
brings small and big trees
down are you trying to kill us
Boss each brittle night
each grim gray day
are you trying to prove
how each breath is a bet won
a wistful guess played out
I bet you taste what you deal out
on the tip of your tongue Boss
the frozen tears that melt
at your lips I bet it hurts you
Boss when another one of us
is trapped outside too far
from home do you ever
feel that way no light in sight
at dusk when you are out looking
Boss out in all that wind
searching for us

4

it's dark outside Boss
dusk to dawn like a river
I can't cross
the far bank covered in mist
is it like that for you Boss
do you ever wish the sun
would hurry up
does the wind ever blow
your door open to a storm
branches flying
trees itching to fall
do you ever let yourself
not know what's going to happen
let yourself be surprised
by the lightning
the way the cardinal sings
its spring-is-coming song
O Boss it makes me want
to sing does it make you
want to sing too does it
make you clear your throat

5

you could have done everything
a lot differently Boss
you could have been louder
maybe prettier Boss
how would I know
all we could ever hear
would be you talking
or maybe see you shining
never stopping to hide
behind a bush or the horizon
how would that be for you Boss
always having to talk
or dress yourself up
never leaning back against a tree
with a stem of grass in your mouth
never letting us stumble around
on a moonless night wondering
if you'll ever turn up again
with only one star at dusk
to say you're still alive

6

what if we knew what would happen
Boss what if we saw trouble just around
the corner beating a path to our door
pounding to be let in sound of heavy
boots what if we'd seen their plan Boss
not just their scribbled orders
brows turned cold strong-arm mean
what if we'd seen your dream candle
in the night bright morning star
ever new hope manger-born
sheep-surrounded all-time turnaround
far shore out of sight but close Boss
so close what if you whispered in our ear
the jig is up cows out of the barn
fire kindled ship set sail what if we knew
how close the new day Boss so close

7

Boss you are the unbossiest Boss I know
no go there get down stop start
shove pull hit Boss
you are a squirrel
speeding up a branch
then stopping to see if I'm with you
step for step it sure seems to me
you're shaking your tail pardon me
Boss but it looks like you're something
of a tease with all your hints
and dropped handkerchiefs
O Boss if I'm out of line
I know you'll nudge me back
maybe place a root for me to trip over
but I swear it looks like you take a shine
to every tree you plant every bush
and flower every single soul of us

8

if you can start a wind
here and stop it there
Boss uproot trees
replant new ones
empty rivers
fill them back up
can you turn a body around
stuck in fifty years ago
face to face
guts in a clutch
if you can fill up valleys
remake mountains Boss
can you shake my eyeballs loose
rattle my brainpan
enough to see
clean out my ears to hear
unloose my arms
unclinch my hands

9

you're not finished are you Boss
I say mountain you say mud
I say rain you say dry well
you're still fiddling with me
tinker here wallop there
was that you yesterday in the swamp
standing on a stump giving me
the hoot-owl eye you asking me
if I was tired of sleep-walking
did I want to see the slow water rise
decade's sea change Boss
you haven't given up have you
silent wingbeats in shadows
head-spin backwards that's when
you find me behind you Boss
looking the other way for dry land
you keep asking me who I think I am

10

I heard you singing yesterday
Boss I heard you at the forest's edge
by the field still fallow from frosts
you bringing your howdy tune
after journeys south you hiding
in the bramble canes belting out
you're here again still a hidey-tail
flash of feathers loud enough
for hope of greeny things
springing from the ground
as yet unseen the way you do
flitting flighty Boss singer
dancer ghost holy maker
bring your song honey-supple
smell buds split open push out
of dirt let life loose again
you were gone but not really
Boss never really Boss

11

some days I want to stomp
my foot Boss so hard
the old leaning chair falls flat
on the floor and scares the cat
out the door when I hear
one mean word too many
in my ear in my heart
in my broke-open heart
you put it in there Boss
you make it soft again
over and over the way
you plough the earth
the way you make it wet
call out the baby plants
maybe even the pointy
stab words burning eyes
crack open my dry ground
soul but I've still got to put
my foot down Boss
I've still got to stomp
so do you I guess you've
got to put your foot down too

1 2

Boss as much as I want
rain or the quiet
that comes after
as much as the daisy bed
whispers my name
or the cardinal winks
from behind his branch
or the new-turned soil
makes me yank off my boots
it's always you
isn't it Boss
you want me to want
and I do and I hurt
sometimes half the time
sometimes all
and the roots keep peeking
out of my heart
sneaking their way
down to my feet
and I'm starting to wonder
Boss if I'm just going
to become a tree

13

people should be people Boss
the way birds need to be birds
and dirt needs to be dirt
why do people try to grow wings
one minute and let themselves be trod
underfoot the next all to get
a handshake or slaphappy smile
as empty as a slop bucket
turned upside down
people need people who need
other people every one of them
as different as each patch
on my grandmother's crazy-quilt
only instead of pretty patterns
we pull each other's hair
snicker behind hands
until we fall down and cry
whether our tears show or not
is that how you want it Boss
all of us lying down
every single different one of us
lying cockeyed in a Babel pile
looking up at you

14

part of the problem Boss
is that
I am
are you
part of the problem
like a racoon running
this way and that
backtracking
or is it just you
keeping us awake
limber loose in love
letting you lead
my eyes cross Boss
ears hurt
some days like today
shake my fist Boss
head snapping back
am I battling with you
or just another neighbor
one more unfamiliar song
or reel I need to join
or parry
new face next door
or two face
is this a fight
or a dance
and is it with him her
or is it with you

15

Boss I thought words were friends
plants in the garden I could watch
gray in winter sprout green
then yellow blue pink to decorate
each day songs with a friend
now they're clods in the air
rocks in a sling slung
at any stranger strange ways
lost children women at our doors
I thought words were hymns
prayers Boss chants poems
shining tools candles to help
hope build bind bear better best
Boss what happened
to nouns verbs supple
subtle vessels for grams
grains gambols at facts
hearts hurts hopes we dance on
stub our toes over Boss
hard one moment soft the next
like each day family nation
person place or thing

16

do you have that little girl
in you Boss that little boy
do they still run in circles
in your head the way
they do in mine doing
somersaults running up the hill
then rolling sideways down
do they get leaves in their hair
mud on their knees
pull on your pants leg
when you're busy hanging
up the sun rearranging
a cloud did you ever lose
one Boss no matter how loud
you yelled how far you roamed
calling her name O come home
baby come home up valleys
down streams from mountaintops
and she never answered
never came home do you
keep looking Boss
keep seeing her pop up
behind a bush or a rock
out the corner of your eye
wanting so bad for her
to step out from behind
some hope-shadowed tree

17

just when I'm done in
Boss the moment my eyes
stop searching the edge of day
and I sink to the kitchen stool
with too many potatoes to peel
for a soup started too late
a knock that never comes
on my door just then Boss
when the unwashed dishes glare
at me the unfinished chores
and I am alone another night
you show up Boss you bubble
in the pot you fill the room
with garlic you blow
through the window crack
and make the candle shadows
shudder and rustle the letter
to the floor and I read your name
again between the lines
as I pick it up and put it back
on the table next to the flame
and you remind me you are
a come-again go-again Boss
with soft arms gentle hands
and a funny bone just like you
Boss to drop by ignoring
the door and my tired eyeballs
you rascal Boss you never stay put

you pull me out of my chair
and make me dance again
you two-step clogging Boss
and then you're off gallivanting
somewhere else my back still warm
from your hands my heart still
hot from your squeeze sometimes
I wish you would just sit still

18

when I slow my breath and look around
I am a bird tree rock Boss
is that the way it is with you
spreading your wings when the sun
breaks from behind a cloud
you adding a new leaf to a branch
or just lying around in glinty quartz
we're family aren't we Boss
you me caterpillar mud
pebble sand raindrop muscadine
goat we're a crazy quilt Boss
catawampus shapes and colors
and you're the thread Boss
you're the needle and thread

19

what about the liars Boss
hoax-makers deceivers
burning wicks low
for taller this bigger that
while they call planters of trees fools
keepers of sheep dreamers
O who will shepherd the soil Boss
who will nurse the barrens
once they are nothing but clay
when I speak up they track me down
study my false steps
they know me well enough
to stick fingers in my wounds
and laugh when I stutter
O pin them with their lies Boss
corral them with truth
so that when you open wide
your door Boss everyone
can breathe again
every vine lamb field forest
every me you them

20

the world is tilty Boss
leans one way in morning
another at dusk
hills edge closer at dawn
draw back at the sun's last gasp
wind all pillow now
then a saw blade bent on doom
it's hard to walk straight
stay true unless Boss unless
your finger's in the muddle
your feet and heart
and you've jumped in
and made so big a splash
I'm a fish beneath the wave
swimming behind your back
I don't know whether
to laugh cry or just swim
all shaky and slant
does your stomach
get in a knot like mine Boss
do you ever just want
to climb out on some beach
or maybe that's what you are too
not just sea but longed-for shore

21

look out your window Boss
see the smoke hear the noise
please get up Boss
the fields are nothing but dust
my cistern smells foul
I cover my nose and mouth
my seed lies idle
yet the fancy-dressed
sit in quiet rooms
lined up in rows
the clean-clothed pray
to their self-made chief
who preaches what they want to hear
knock their steeples down
Boss turn over their pews
break their dams
their walled-in reservoirs
let new vines sprout again
make fruit tree branches bend
look out your window Boss
make our fields fertile with your tears

22

the hoot owl Boss
yellow-breasted chat
is that you
looking for conversation
Boss the redbud popping open
dogwood bloodroot
hankering for a face-to-face
do you get miffed
when I don't notice
thumbs in my suspenders
like I've got
better things to do
is that you waving your hands
dust devils rock slides Boss
honeysuckle on every fence post
you getting lonely
our eyes shut ears plugged can't smell

23

the vireo is back Boss
wearing her yellow spectacles
loud as a jay shy as a colt
a hide and seeker like you Boss
close as grass under my feet
but secret like its roots
am I walking on your chest
right now Boss are my feet
tickling your belly
is the birdsong your voice
or is it your way of keeping me
guessing we're two peas
in a pod Boss chirping
at each other playing peekaboo

24

how do I say thank you Boss
how dance my nobody's-looking
steps clap hands tap feet
yell in woods sing in fields
plough another row pull weeds
wish you had hands Boss
fingers I could hold
you'd flip me over
I'd say do it again
dancing Boss you and me
hide-and-seek until nightfall
some summer dusk
it's coming Boss the longest day
of the year I'm waiting Boss
katydid and tree frog beats
tickle hands itchy feet

25

it's the birds I like best
Boss the warble wake sunsong
cloudspeck dropdown hawkflight
tree-alive branch-dance
O Boss one day to skyprance
the air's soft hand beneath
to turn some way
not so often down
but over out around
I love my feet Boss
mudboots shovel earth
rock piles crawly vines
yet sunwise clouds call
and don't all growers
hanker higher
can't we earthbounds
crave bright wings
don't bent heads seek
lighter loads wild and free

26

you're the spring
and the pond Boss
clear on a sunny day
trout lounging in shallows
you well up from darkness
unshaped hours
I'm a dragonfly
just over the surface
with zippy moves
I sip as I can
your slow beats my fast
every time Boss
but don't my purple wings
show off your glossy deep

27

do you feel old Boss
does the sun hit
your eyes wrong
late in the afternoon
does somebody say
you're not doing it right
one time too many
the roar and whine
stick to you like spider webs
loam turned to dust
is there a quiet room
in your house where
two or three
make it three
sit around the fire
and talk quietly
pass some kind of jug
O Boss I hope so
this night
this tired night

28

you are the wind Boss
you sift my hand
I open my fingers
and you pass through
I close them and my arm
kicks back at the mountain's edge
then you're nowhere to be felt
nothing but stillness
me left with bees in my head
my hat too tight eyes turned in
and a belly that can't make up
its mind I know you want me
to sit still but my feet want to run
I'm hoping Boss
just waiting
for one leaf to stir
one branch to bend

29

do you admit we're your own
Boss third cousins
once removed or twice
long-lost relatives
from some faraway town
nobody's ever heard of
even the people who live there
the part of the family
unspoken unnamed
unfashioned or yet to be
the object of your smile
you do smile sometimes
don't you Boss
surely when we're born
or when we see that one bloom
in the corner of the field
yellow with shiny bracts
and don't pick it
but just admire
surely then Boss

30

here's how I see it Boss
stars are the clue aren't they
you're not just everything
down here
smack and wash of sea
sumac's stink
beech tree's balm
sandstone stairs
streaked quartz
fox feet
king snake slink
honeysuckle sap
blood in our veins
you're up there as well
Boss not just in clouds
or in sunstream
but when it's darkest
you're one star here
then there then wishbone
stinger bow horse crown
bull bear crab
all of them Boss
free-flying open
O Boss empty open
thank you
space

3 1

if I'd felt any lower Boss
I'd have been a salamander
maybe or the bottom end
of a hickory root I was lonelier
than the last ivory-billed
but you picked me up Boss
shook the dirt out of my hair
spat on my eyes and poured
something stronger than coffee
made my knees straight again
gave me a little shove
from behind and said
go ahead set those feet free

32

sometimes there's a rooster in my head
Boss thinks he knows everybody
better than they know themselves
earlier as well
gets next to my mouth and spouts
like a fountain I can't cut off
cock of the walk
won't shut up
why'd you let him in
Boss to turn me inside-out
into a pants-down fool
why give me now and then
a good idea if he can swoop
down and tie a string around it
the other end to my finger
so I think it's mine
I don't own anything do I Boss
I don't own one blessed thing

33

the birds must have slipped off
last night Boss must have heard
the north wind turn this way
to lay silence over all the hills
the ground tucked into its new
feather bed and I am the only thing
I can hear this morning the only one
do you ever wake up
to no puff of air Boss
no fresh tracks on the trail
just the sound of your heart
or was it only that one first time
and ever since it's something
anything everything every day
on the hunt prowl or maybe
just lonesome but O Boss
these sun-sparkly hills
and ring-fingered trees
unblinking air and earth at rest
they are all part of you aren't they
not just waiting but resting Boss
every thing and every one of us
even you listening to your heart

3 4

if it's not too much trouble
Boss could you just look
over this way while the geese
are passing before the setting moon
and the wind riffles oak leaves
could you spare a glance
they're putting children in pens
Boss they're telling the mothers
to wait in cities and towns
they're calling for trust with keys
in their hands and locks in their minds
so if you could just put your ear
to the gate and peer through the fence
maybe a spring might grow
to a creek might swell to a run
might rush in a flood to knock down
the dam and break up the wall
not just at our edges but in our souls

35

you know how I daydream Boss
how I stop washing dishes
grow wings on my back
and fly around the yard
maybe over to that mountain
with the slickrock face
and burley tree-freckles
or over to so-and-so's house
the one I love but who sticks
his foot out to trip my mind
I'll bet you're a daydreamer too
urging birds to laugh at clouds
and beavers to slap their tails
at each other's jokes
you sure are funny dreaming
us into whoever it is we are
maybe you could let us in
on your dreams Boss
maybe slap your tail
for me and my friend

36

Boss can I only dance
with my feet
their leap spin flat-foot
buck maybe add
arms and hands
like the dogwood tree's
barest branches with blooms
or can a song make
the floor shake by itself
or the smell of new bread
or a joke told by my daughter
and can a sketch scratched
into window ice
be a footfree ballet
a well-hewn word
intake of breath
or simply the ready
unseen but steady
faithful dancemaster
beat of my heart

37

what would I do Boss
if there were no you
no one to swirl fog
through cuts and swales
tilt the earth
whistle in forests
teach wolves how to howl
hawks how to do their mating dance
who would I talk to
bicker whimper and guffaw with
could anyone ever dream you up
sew you together
whittle you into shape
no nothings could ever
touch the echo
of you not here
so lonely no thought
could kiss itself into a word
O Boss no hair on my head
no blink of my eye
but you put them there

38

are the vultures facing out or in
Boss they surround my country
like a winged fence
someone has declared that you say
they are here to protect me
wearing their uniforms
carrying subtle clubs
yet the enemy has a face
like my own with eyes darting
this way and that
and why do the raptors' nostrils flare
when they look inside the circle
but not the other way

39

tell me this Boss please
how a blind man
can swear he sees
or that night can be called day
spittle termed a hug
they're building walls
within walls Boss
there's not enough wheat
not enough corn they say
so they shackle the harvester
and shadow the sun
their fires fill the air
their waste the water
they salt the soil
don't they know evil
when they see it
don't they know
anything at all

40

I keep trying to find it Boss
the stream with the boulder
on the side of the hill
the stone that hid me
from the trail below
hemlocks offering cover
and glimpses of whatever
or whoever passed
beside the creek
with its own rocks
disturbing redirecting the flow
the way the mountains alter
the wind the way my body
interrupts the space of others
the way theirs interrupts mine
I keep searching for that pocket
in the woods by the waters
in the mountains where it was dark
and quiet enough to see and hear
underneath my skin and beneath that
of water wind and earth
so often separating and joining
at once different
yet always the same

41

the sun has been up for hours
Boss and I'm just sitting here
watching clouds pass over
my neighbor's roof
I never knew I liked clouds
rolling out a new day
like waves resculpting a beach
and even though it's ordinary
the roof next door speaks comfort
as does my own when it rains
drumming so loud night demons
are too frightened to dance
I never knew I loved roofs
I didn't know I liked my neighbor
the one I argued with the first time
we met the one I tied string around
after I rolled him up like a scroll
and put him on a shelf in my mind
when all each of us wanted
was to help I didn't know I had
to wait years to see how much
I love what's outside my window
my neighbor our roofs and clouds

42

is it just about the well-hoed row
Boss the well-thrown pot or if the hand
on the ladle trembles and spills some soup
does your breath catch do you stop
and take note if my love-words come out
sounding like hate or worse as if I don't care
even though I mostly want to shine the sun
in a broken heart on my decent days
am I always meant to drop crockery
stumble into my neighbor causing her
to fall do you keep count Boss
of all my backward thoughts let alone
the mean ones as if I were in my boyhood
skin and ready to break whatever toy
my best friend holds precious in her hands
do you weigh me in your balance
and find me wanting Boss or do you
want me in your arms waiting
to be slowly turned toward the sun

43

when I was born you breathed
a story in my ear Boss
a tale too tall to take in
of jasmine and dogwood paths
carrion crows
and the fat-tailed fox
your whispered words
were water and fire
that made me reach
for embrace yet howl
for escape Boss will we
always tussle in a four-footed
tug of war and love
I smell you around the corner
your coffin bearers in tow
oh are those lilacs behind your back

44

so many odes to lions and deer
so many love songs
for those with fair hair
but what of the centipede Boss
weevil or midge dogfish
or buzzard hyena or mole
I knew a man with a twisty back
and twistier mouth
a girl with a purple bloom
on her cheek a boy
whose half-pale face
cracked open a door
how many sweet tunes
for the specks we call germs
how many hymns Boss to each one

45

o yes Boss to the question
can I pray without words
aren't my eyes winged cherubs
my nose a seraph
hovering by honeysuckle
my ears a chalice and paten
tuned to the rush of wind
and how can mountains declaim
if confined to poor syllables
or the hickory the oak
don't the very stones
make known your name
by their weight
hail pelting the earth
the paper wasp returned
to build another house
the waterspout
the unending desert
the even vaster sky
the eyes of all wait
on you Boss
they wait

46

I've started remembering Boss
there's a new window in my head
I can see my mother
teasing a kitten with string
my father smoking his pipe
my brother running in the yard
it's the smell of death
that does it Boss
rumors and wide eyes
this morning the sun broke
into my room
like a happy thief
inviting me to ransack my life
a shipload of friends
calling my name
and that laughter
that no one can stop
yanked me out of bed
that was you wasn't it Boss
you and your funny-bone
your strange monkeyshines

47

sometimes they are in my gut
Boss houses caving in
people running this way and that
sometimes it's just inside my ear
a voice that says fly
get out while you can
on occasion my legs refuse
to move or stand straight
something new is afoot
the sky turns dark
pillars snap gates break off
rivers flood then run dry
what I can't sort out Boss
is this bad news or good

48

this place Boss
made of pine trees palmettos
swamp grass and sand
is your current interpreter
of things subtle and soft
uncertain ground
full of dampness and salt
but how I miss mountains
water cutting stone
boulders daring trees
to put down roots
scope and scale of heights
whether sand or stone
does water weather all
our ending and start

49

today Boss it's everything
cypress tree branches
wearing new clothes
next to tupelo boughs
both saying thank you
to pluff mud currency
blackwater swamp
in turn saying hi
to the back-and-forth creek
washing in dolphins
crawdads and crabs
all part of the waltz
looked over by ospreys
warblers and wrens
can it all be you
Boss of the water world
can I take a turn
here in my canoe

50

if I didn't know you better
Boss some days I'd say
you're too busy
to think about me
one leaf on a bush
speck of soil on a boot
hair on a head
while tree-ripping
house-rending wind
turns my village upside down
is that the way you like me
Boss hanging by my tail
like a possum
is that how I can catch
a glimpse of you
is that what it takes
to convince me
that even as a leaf
on a storm-thrashed shrub
I'm not just a plant
but your precious kin

51

once long ago
I was seven smooth stones
in a stream Boss
as if to say to the water
go this way
as if I had substance
last night I was an eon of water
and I laughed while I gurgled
as did the stones
as do you

ACKNOWLEDGMENTS

"it's dark outside Boss" and "are you against me Boss" appeared in *Christianity and Literature*, June, 2020.

A number of these poems have been included in the monthly newsletters of Grace Episcopal Cathedral, Charleston, South Carolina.

Made in the USA
Coppell, TX
19 September 2021

62437626R00039